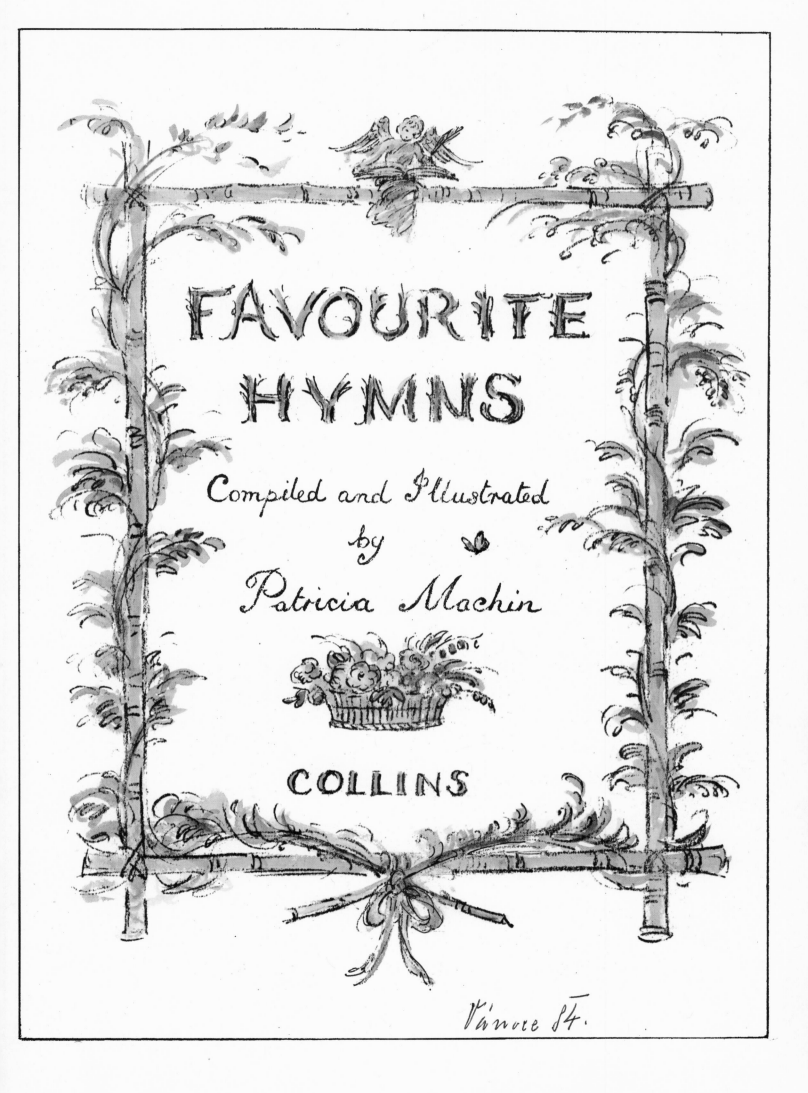

FAVOURITE HYMNS

Compiled and Illustrated
by
Patricia Machin

COLLINS

Vánoce 84.

William Collins Sons & Co Ltd
London · Glasgow · Sydney · Auckland
Toronto · Johannesburg

British Library Cataloguing in Publication Data

Machin, Patricia

   Favourite Hymns.
   1. Hymns, English
   I. Title
   264.2   BV459

   ISBN 0 00 215249 5

The melody of Martin Shaw's arrangement
of 'All Things Bright and Beautiful' is reprinted
by permission of J. Curwen & Sons Ltd, London and
'Morning has Broken' by Eleanor Farjeon is
reprinted by permission of David Higham Associates
Ltd, London.

First published 1981
© Patricia Machin 1981

Made and printed in Great Britain
by W. S. Cowell Ltd, Ipswich

INTRODUCTION

Some hymns are outpourings of reverence and praise by great poets who can condense into a few lines a lifetime of feeling and devotion; "Let all the world in every corner sing" by George Herbert is one. Some are the passionate prayers of great men often at moments of crisis of the soul, such as "Lead, Kindly Light" by Cardinal Newman.

Then there are the hymns written in obscure country vicarages by clergymen who had no desire for fame or fortune, but simply to express their faith. This they have done time and time again, and we are the richer for their creative thought which has channelled the eternal message, each time with new power, into our lives, enriching our Christian heritage and giving us fresh expression of it. John Keble was one of these clergymen; his memorable lines from "Sun of my soul" —
'Abide with me from morn to eve, for without Thee I cannot live;'
'Abide with me when night is nigh, for without Thee I dare not die'
seem to engrave themselves onto the mind as the complete apology of the Christian.

Some hymns contain lines which express not fear but an imaginative awe of the unknown which endear the writers to us. Tennyson wrote (in "Sunset and Evening Star") 'For though from out this bourne of time and place the flood may bear me far, I hope to see my Pilot face to face when I have crost the bar,' and Toplady writes 'When I soar through tracts unknown, see Thee on Thy Judgment Throne, Rock of Ages cleft for me let me hide myself in Thee.'

The scholars who have devoted their lives to the translation of hymns so that they can be included in our hymn books should not be forgotten. Then there are the hymns written in times of great religious unrest by poets such as Charles Wesley and John Bunyan; and many highly original hymns written specifically for the young which remain dear to generations of children.

But above all hymns are prayers of thanksgiving handed down to us through the ages, such as "Jesus Christ is risen today, Alleluia!", an old hymn whose author is unknown which gladdens and uplifts us every Easter, and Isaac Watts's "Jesus shall reign where'er the sun doth his successive journeys run, His Kingdom stretch from shore to shore, till moons shall wax and wane no more" which gives us continual joyous affirmation of Christ's presence on earth for ever.

It is my hope that my attempt in this book to honour a few of our great hymn writers will give pleasure to its readers.

Patricia Machin

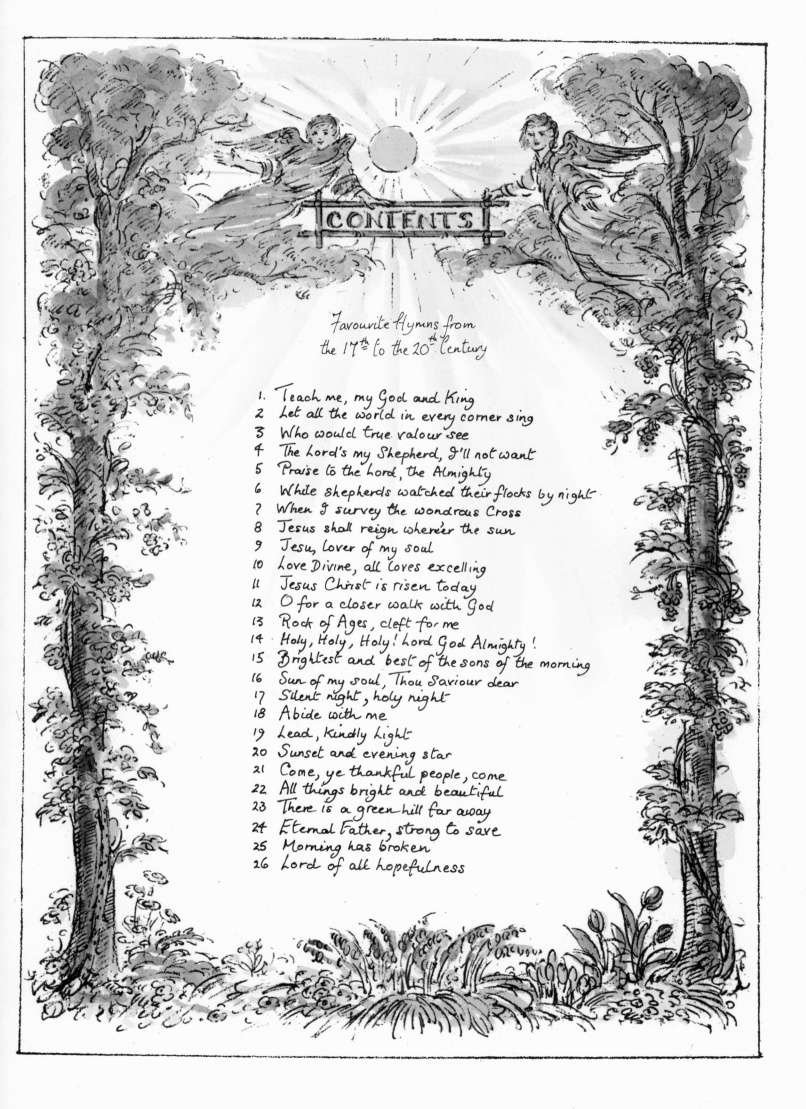

CONTENTS

Favourite Hymns from
the 17th to the 20th Century

GEORGE HERBERT
1593 – 1633

Some of the finest religious poems in existence have been written by George Herbert. He was born at Montgomery Castle, Wales into an aristocratic family; his older brother, Lord Edward Herbert, was himself a poet and philosopher, while his mother was one of the brilliant intellectual ladies of the period.

Herbert was a pupil at Westminster School, and after studying at Cambridge he was elected the University's Public Orator. He was highly esteemed by James I and by great men such as Bacon and Donne, but forsook his life as a fashionable courtier to become a country clergyman.

English Carol Melody – 1

THE ELIXIR
BY
GEORGE HERBERT

Teach me, my God and King,
  In all things Thee to see,
And what I do in anything
  To do it as for Thee.

A man that looks on glass
  On it may stay his eye;
Or if he pleaseth, through it pass,
  And then the heaven espy.

All may of Thee partake:
  Nothing can be so mean,
Which with his tincture 'For Thy sake'
  Will not grow bright and clean.

A servant with this clause
  Makes drudgery divine:
Who sweeps a room, as for Thy laws,
  Makes that and the action fine.

This is the famous stone
  That turneth all to gold:
For that which God doth touch and own
  Cannot for less be told.

GEORGE HERBERT
1593 – 1633

After taking holy orders Herbert accepted the living of Bemerton, Wiltshire, where he died three years later at the early age of forty. The Temple, a collection of his religious poems, was published in 1633. His chief prose work, A Priest to the Temple, described by Izaac Walton as containing 'plain, prudent, useful rules for the country parson', was first printed in 1652. Walton concluded his life of Herbert (which appeared in 1670) with these words:

'Thus he liv'd, and thus he dy'd like a Saint, unspotted of the World, full of Alms-deeds, full of Humility, and all the examples of a vertuous life'.

Basil Harwood
(1859 – 1949)

ANTIPHON BY GEORGE HERBERT

Let all the world in every corner sing
          My God and King!

  The heavens are not too high,
  His praise may thither fly;
  The earth is not too low
  His praises there may grow.

Let all the world in every corner sing
          My God and King!

  The church with psalms must shout,
  No door can keep them out;
  But above all the heart
  Must bear the longest part.

Let all the world in every corner sing
          My God and King!

1628   JOHN BUNYAN   1688

Although Bunyan was the son of a poor tinker and without formal education, he wrote with much grace of language. He felt himself compelled to preach the gospel, and in 1660 was thrown into Bedford gaol because he did not belong to the state church under Charles II. He was not liberated for twelve years but spent the time writing religious works. Three years later he again suffered imprisonment but for six months only, during which time he wrote the first part of Pilgrim's Progress, the fame of which during his lifetime was immense.

English Folk Song

A PILGRIM'S HYMN
BY JOHN BUNYAN

Who would true valour see,
Let him come hither;
One here will constant be,
Come wind, come weather.
There's no discouragement
Shall make him once relent
His first avowed intent
　　To be a pilgrim.

Whoso beset him round
With dismal stories,
Do but themselves confound;
His strength the more is.
No lion can him fright,
He'll with a giant fight
But he will have a right
　　To be a pilgrim.

Hobgoblin nor foul fiend
Can daunt his spirit;
He knows he at the end
Shall life inherit.
Then fancies fly away;
He'll not fear what men say;
He'll labour night and day
　　To be a pilgrim.

1650

SCOTTISH PSALTER

When the Reformation came to Scotland and the psalms in the metrical versions were sung, Psalm 23 was high among the favourites.

There have been many versions of this psalm; George Herbert wrote "The God of Love my Shepherd is"; Isaac Watts wrote "My Shepherd will supply my need", and Sir H.W. Baker, the prolific hymn writer who edited Hymns Ancient and Modern (the first comprehensive hymn book of the Church of England) wrote "The King of Love my Shepherd is".

The popularity of the version chosen here greatly increased after it was sung at Princess Elizabeth's wedding in 1947.

Jessie Seymour Irvine
(1836–87)

A HYMN OF THANKSGIVING

The Lord's my Shepherd, I'll not want.
He makes me down to lie
In pastures green: He leadeth me
The quiet waters by.

My soul He doth restore again,
And me to walk doth make
Within the paths of righteousness,
Ev'n for His own Name's sake.

Yea, though I walk in death's dark vale,
Yet will I fear none ill:
For Thou art with me; and Thy rod
And staff me comfort still.

My table Thou hast furnished
In presence of my foes;
My head Thou dost with oil anoint
And my cup overflows.

Goodness and mercy all my life
Shall surely follow me:
And in God's house for evermore
My dwelling place shall be.

4

1650-1680
JOACHIM NEANDER
Translated by
CATHERINE WINKWORTH 1827-1878

Born at Bremen, Neander was a schoolmaster and was rebuked by the Church Elders for not conforming to the Reformed Church and for starting separate prayer meetings. For this reason he had to leave both school and town, and for some months lived in a cave near the Rhine. Known as the first poet of the Reformed Church in Germany, he is also famous for the tunes he wrote to go with his poems. The fourth verse is not by Neander; it was added later, but I include it for its vividly descriptive quality which I find very appealing.

A HYMN OF PRAISE

Praise to the Lord, the Almighty, the King of creation!
O my soul, praise Him, for he is thy health and salvation!
All ye who hear,
Now to his temple draw near,
Join me in glad adoration.

Praise to the Lord, who o'er all things so wondrously reigneth,
Shelters thee under His Wings, yea, so gently sustaineth:
Hast thou not seen
How thy desires have been
Granted in what he ordaineth?

Praise to the Lord who doth prosper thy work and defend thee,
Surely His goodness and mercy here daily attend thee:
Ponder anew
What the Almighty can do
If with His love he befriend thee.

Praise to the Lord, who when darkness of sin is abounding,
Who, when the godless do triumph, all virtue confounding,
Sheddeth his light;
Chaseth the horrors of night,
Saints with His mercy surrounding.

Praise to the Lord! Oh let all that is in me adore Him!
All that hath life and breath come now with praises before Him!
Let the Amen
Sound from His people again,
Gladly for aye we adore Him!

NAHUM TATE
1652 ~ 1715

Two Irish clergymen, Nicolas Brady and Nahum Tate, published in 1696 a <u>New Version of the Psalms</u> which was considered more poetical than the 'Old Version' which it gradually supplanted; its simple dignity and lyrical power has endeared it to generations of worshippers. Four years later a supplement was added to the New Version, together with six hymns, one of which was this poetical account of the Nativity. More hymns were added in further supplements as it had proved very popular; this greatly encouraged the use of hymns in the Established Church. Tate later became Poet Laureate.

A CHRISTMAS HYMN

While shepherds watched their flocks by night,
    All seated on the ground,
The angel of the Lord came down,
    And glory shone around.

'Fear not', said he: for mighty dread
    Had seized their troubled mind;
'Glad tidings of great joy I bring
    To you and all mankind.'

'To you in David's town this day
    Is born of David's line
A saviour who is Christ the Lord:
    And this shall be the sign:'

'The heavenly Babe you there shall find
    To human view display'd,
All meanly wrapp'd in swathing bands,
    And in a manger laid.'

Thus spake the seraph: and forthwith
    Appear'd a shining throng
Of angels praising God, who thus
    Address'd their joyful song:

'All glory be to God on high,
    And to the earth be peace;
Good will henceforth from Heav'n to men
    Begin and never cease.'

ISAAC WATTS

1674 - 1748

The eldest of nine children, Watts was
born at Southampton where his father was a
schoolmaster who was twice imprisoned for his
nonconformist religious convictions. Watts himself refused
a university education (which was only open to Anglicans)
and instead attended the Dissenter Academy of Thomas Rowe,
later becoming a minister at Mark Lane Chapel. His health
was not good and Sir Thomas Abney invited him for a visit
to Theobalds, Hertfordshire where he remained as tutor and
private chaplain for the last thirty-six years of his life.

It was in this liberal and happy atmosphere that most of his
hymns were written. Watts is known as the father of hymnody and
this hymn is often pronounced the finest in the English language.

arr. Edward Miller
(1735 - 1807)

A HYMN FOR THE PASSION

When I survey the wondrous Cross
On which the Prince of glory died,
My richest gain I count but loss
And pour contempt on all my pride.

Forbid it, Lord, that I should boast
Save in the death of Christ my God;
All the vain things that charm me most
I sacrifice them to His blood.

See from His head, His hands, His feet
Sorrow and love flow mingled down;
Did e'er such love and sorrow meet
Or thorns compose so rich a crown?

Were the whole realm of nature mine,
That were a present far too small;
Love so amazing, so divine,
Demands my soul, my life, my all.

ISAAC WATTS
1674 — 1748

Known as the father of English hymnody,
Watts wrote over six hundred hymns.

Before his time hymns were rarely sung
in public worship. It is said that after complaining
to his father that the psalmody at the chapel
service was not interesting enough he produced
his first hymn "Behold the Glories of the Lamb" for
the service on the following sunday.

It was so favourably received he was
asked to compose another one for the next sunday
and he brought a fresh one each week until a
whole volume was formed.

Ralph Harrison
(1748 – 1810)

A HYMN IN CELEBRATION OF THE KINGDOM OF CHRIST

Jesus shall reign where'er the sun
Doth his successive journeys run;
His Kingdom stretch from shore to shore,
Till moons shall wax and wane no more.

People and realms of every tongue
Dwell on his love with sweetest song,
And infant voices shall proclaim
Their early blessings on His name

Blessings abound where'er He reigns;
The prisoner leaps to lose his chains;
The weary find eternal rest,
And all the sons of want are blest.

Let every creature rise and bring
Peculiar honours to our King;
Angels descend with songs again,
And earth repeat the loud Amen.

CHARLES WESLEY
1707 - 1788

Admirers of Wesley's hymns may not realize that he was also a brilliant classical scholar. Under his brother Samuel at Westminster School and at Oxford (where he was later to become a tutor) he received a complete classical education, with insistance on such subjects as rhetoric which are regarded as unimportant today. This knowledge, together with his poetic gift and his sense of spiritual urgency resulted in the hymns for which he is known as the poet of Methodism

Joseph Parry
(1841-1903)

A HYMN for THOSE in TROUBLED WATERS

Jesu, Lover of my soul,
Let me to Thy bosom fly,
While the nearer waters roll,
While the tempest still is high:
Hide me, O my Saviour, hide,
Till the storm of Life is past;
Safe into the haven guide,
O receive my soul at last.

Other refuge have I none:
Hangs my helpless soul on Thee;
Leave, ah! leave me not alone,
Still support and comfort me.
All my trust on Thee is stay'd,
All my help from Thee I bring;
Cover my defenceless head
With the shadow of Thy wing.

Plenteous grace with Thee is found,
Grace to cover all my sin;
Let the healing streams abound;
Make and keep me pure within;
Thou of life the fountain art;
Freely let me take of Thee;
Spring Thou up within my heart,
Rise to all eternity.

CHARLES WESLEY
1707 – 1788

Charles Wesley was born in Epworth Rectory in Lincolnshire. While he was at Christchurch, Oxford, he founded, with his brother John, the Methodist movement. Whilst John, travelling on horseback, preached in the open air all over England with amazing energy and depth of purpose, Charles had an equally powerful influence as a poet, composing over six thousand hymns. It is said that over forty different passages from the scriptures can be traced in this hymn. It has become widely used at wedding services although when Wesley wrote it he never intended it for this purpose.

John Stainer
(1840–1901)

A HYMN FOR WEDDINGS

Love Divine all love excelling,
  Joy of Heav'n to earth come down,
Fix in us Thy humble dwelling,
  All Thy faithfull mercies crown.

Jesu, Thou art all compassion,
  Pure unbounded love Thou art;
Visit us with Thy salvation,
  Enter every trembling heart.

Come, Almighty to deliver,
  Let us all Thy grace receive;
Suddenly return, and never,
  Never more Thy temples leave.

Thee we would be always blessing
  Serve Thee as Thy Hosts above;
Pray, and praise Thee without ceasing,
  Glory in Thy perfect love.

Finish then Thy new creation,
  Pure and spotless let us be;
Let us see Thy great salvation
  Perfectly restored in Thee.

Changed from glory into glory
  Till in Heav'n we take our place,
Till we cast our crowns before Thee
  Lost in wonder, love and praise.

Charles Wesley
(1707 – 88)

ANONYMOUS

The author and translator of
this hymn are unknown but it is said
to have originated as an Easter card in the
fourteenth century. The tune comes from the
book called _Lyra Davidica_ published in 1708.
It is fitting that "Alleluia!" is introduced at the
end of each line as this word was the recognized
Easter salutation in the early Christian Church
and means 'Praise ye the Lord;' it can be traced
back to temple worship in Old Testament times.

Lyra Davidica
(1708)

EASTER DAY

Jesus Christ is risen today
> Alleluia!

Our triumphant holy day
> Alleluia!

Who did once upon the cross
> Alleluia!

Suffer to redeem our loss
> Alleluia!

Hymns of praise then let us sing
> Alleluia!

Unto Christ our heavenly King
> Alleluia!

Who endured the cross and grave
> Alleluia!

Sinners to redeem and save
> Alleluia!

But the pains which he endured
> Alleluia!

Our salvation have procured
> Alleluia!

Now above the sky He's King
> Alleluia!

Where the angels ever sing
> Alleluia!

WILLIAM COWPER
1731 – 1800

The son of the chaplain to George II, Cowper was born at the Rectory of Berkhamstead. He became famous in his lifetime for such poems as "The Task" and "John Gilpin".

While living at Olney, Buckinghamshire, he wrote over sixty hymns at the instigation of his friend the vicar, the Rev. John Newton, a reformed slave trader who also wrote hymns. Cowper suffered from severe mental depression and during these times he found consolation in his love of animals. He wrote many poems about them, one of the best known being "Epitaph on a Hare" written on the death of his pet hare, Tiney.

Scottish Psalter (1635)

WALKING WITH GOD
by
WILLIAM COWPER

O for a closer walk with God,
A calm and heavenly frame;
A light to shine upon the road
That leads me to the Lamb!

What peaceful hours I once enjoyed!
How sweet their memory still!
But they have left an aching void
The world can never fill.

Return, O Holy Dove, return,
Sweet messenger of rest:
I hate the sins that made Thee mourn
And drove Thee from my breast.

The dearest idol I have known,
Whate'er that idol be,
Help me to tear it from Thy throne
And worship only Thee.

So shall my walk be close with God,
Calm and serene my frame,
So purer light shall mark the road
That leads me to the Lamb.

1740 – 1778

AUGUSTUS MONTAGUE TOPLADY

Because Toplady was curate of the Parish of Blagdon
on the Mendips it has been said that he wrote this hymn
when sheltering from a thunderstorm in Burrington
Combe, in the heart of the Mendip Range, but there is
no evidence to support this legend.

The hymn was first published in 1776, only two
years before the author's death at the early age of
thirty-eight.

During the reign of Queen Victoria this hymn was
very popular; it was a great favourite of Mr. Gladstone,
her Prime Minister, who translated it into Latin, Greek
and Italian.   The Prince Consort is said to have
spoken it as he lay dying.

Richard Redhead.
(1820–1901)

A HYMN for
FORGIVENESS

Rock of ages cleft for me,
Let me hide myself in thee;
Let the water and the blood
From Thy riven Side which flowed
Be of sin the double cure,
Cleanse me from its guilt and power.

Not the labours of my hands
Can fulfil Thy law's demands;
Could my zeal no respite know,
Could my tears for ever flow
All for sin could not atone,
Thou must save and Thou alone.

Nothing in my hand I bring,
Simply to Thy Cross I cling,
Naked, come to Thee for dress;
Helpless, look to Thee for grace;
Foul, I to the fountain fly;
Wash me, Saviour, or I die.

While I draw this fleeting breath,
When my eyelids close in death,
When I soar through tracts unknown,
See Thee on Thy judgment throne,
Rock of ages, cleft for me,
Let me hide myself in Thee.

1783 BISHOP HEBER 1826

During the sixteen years Heber was rector of Hodnet in Shropshire he composed many hymns and this was his finest, with its ageless quality and emphasis on the holiness of God. It was the poet Tennyson's favourite hymn and was sung at his funeral. Heber was made Bishop of Calcutta in 1823 and died three years later at the early age of forty-three in Trichinopoly. His diocese consisted of the whole of British India together with Australasia so it is not surprising that he did not survive long.

John Bacchus Dykes
(1823-76)

A HYMN OF WORSHIP

Holy, Holy, Holy! Lord God Almighty!
Early in the morning our song shall rise to Thee:
Holy, Holy, Holy! Merciful and Mighty!
God in Three Persons, Blessèd Trinity!

Holy, Holy, Holy! all the saints adore Thee,
Casting down their golden crowns around the glassy sea;
Cherubim and Seraphim falling down before Thee,
Which wert, and art, and evermore shalt be.

Holy, Holy, Holy! though the darkness hide Thee,
Though the eye of sinful man Thy glory may not see,
Only Thou art Holy, there is none beside Thee
Perfect in power, in love, and purity.

Holy, Holy, Holy! Lord God Almighty!
All Thy works shall praise Thy name, in earth and sky and sea:
Holy, Holy, Holy! Merciful and Mighty!
God in Three Persons, Blessèd Trinity!

BISHOP HEBER
1783 · 1826

Reginald Heber gave up a quiet life as a country clergyman to become a missionary in India. Of his fifty-seven hymns at least half a dozen are still in use.

One of his best known, "From Greenland's Icy Mountains" was written in twenty minutes on the Saturday before Whitsunday in 1819 at the request of his father-in-law, the vicar of Wrexham, who needed a suitable hymn for his sermon the next day, when a collection was to be made for the Society for the Propagation for the Gospel.

German arr. J.S. Bach (1685-1750)

A Hymn for Epiphany

Brightest and best of the sons of the morning,
Dawn on our darkness and lend us thine aid !
Star of the East, the horizon adorning,
Guide where our infant Redeemer is laid !

Cold on His cradle the dewdrops are shining,
Low lies His head with the beasts of the stall;
Angels adore Him in slumber reclining,
Maker and Monarch and Saviour of all.

Say, shall we yield Him in costly devotion,
Odours of Edom and offerings divine?
Gems of the mountain, and pearls of the ocean,
Myrrh from the forest, or gold from the mine ?

Vainly we offer each ample oblation,
Vainly with gifts would this favour secure;
Richer by far is the heart's adoration,
Dearer to God are the prayers of the poor.

JOHN KEBLE

1792 - 1866

The son of a country clergyman, Keble was born at Fairford in Gloucestershire. At the early age of fifteen he went to Oxford where he was a brilliant scholar. Although he was appointed Professor of Poetry he was never quite at home in Oxford and in 1835 accepted the living of Hursley, a village six miles from Winchester, where he stayed for the rest of his working life.

Although much of his time was spent in writing (he was one of the leaders of the Oxford, or Tractarian, Movement) his parishioners loved their quiet, unassuming vicar who was constant in his ministry to them.

Herbert Oakeley
(1830 – 1903)

A HYMN AT NIGHTIME

Sun of my soul, Thou Saviour dear,
It is not night if Thou be near;
O may no earth-born cloud arise
To hide Thee from Thy servant's eyes.

When the soft dews of kindly sleep
My wearied eyelids gently steep,
Be my last thought, how sweet to rest
For ever on my Saviour's breast.

Abide with me from morn till eve,
For without Thee I cannot live;
Abide with me when night is nigh,
For without Thee I dare not die.

If some poor wandering child of Thine
Have spurned today the voice Divine,
Now, Lord, the gracious work begin,
Let him no more lie down in sin.

Watch by the sick; enrich the poor
With blessings from Thy boundless store;
Be every mourner's sleep tonight
Like infant's slumbers, pure and light.

Come near and bless us when we wake,
Ere through the world our way we take;
Till in the ocean of Thy love
We lose ourselves in Heaven above.

JOSEPH MOHR
1792 – 1848

Born in Salzburg, Joseph Mohr was a boy chorister in the Cathedral. In 1815 he was ordained into the Roman Catholic priesthood and became assistant priest in the Bavarian village of Oberdorf. Here, on 24th December 1818 he asked Franz Grüber the organist to set the words of this carol to music, and it was sung that very night at Midnight Mass. It was very much popularized in Britain by American troops in the 1939-45 War.

Franz Grüber (1787-1863)

A
HYMN
for
CHRISTMAS

Silent night, holy night :
All is calm, all is bright
Round the Virgin Mother and Child .
Holy Infant, so tender and mild,
Sleep in heavenly peace,
Sleep in heavenly peace.

Silent night, holy night :
Shepherds quake at the sight ;
Glories stream from heaven afar,
Heavenly hosts sing "Alleluia";
"Christ the Saviour is born,
"Christ the Saviour is born.

Silent night, holy night:
Wondrous star, lend your light;
With the angels let us sing
Alleluia to our King;
Christ our Saviour is born,
Christ our Saviour is born.

HENRY FRANCIS LYTE
1793 ~ 1847

Lyte was born at Ednam, Kelso, on the
Scottish border, and at first intended to join
the medical profession, but changed his mind and
was ordained at the age of twenty-three. He was
vicar of Brixham, in Devon, for nearly twenty-five
years, where he was much loved by his seafaring
parishioners. Never very strong, he was ordered by his
doctors to spend the winter of 1847 in the South of France.
In the summer of that year he wrote this hymn, and on
Sunday, September 4th, in very poor health, after addressing
his parishioners for the last time, he is said to have handed the
final version of it to his daughter-in-law, after spending the
calm of the evening in his garden. A few days later he
left for Nice, where he died on November 20th.

William Henry Monk
(1823-1889)

EVENING

Abide with me; fast falls the eventide;
The darkness deepens: Lord, with me abide;
When other helpers fail, and comforts flee,
Help of the helpless, O abide with me.

Swift to its close ebbs out life's little day;
Earth's joys grow dim, its glories pass away;
Change and decay in all around I see;
O Thou who changest not, abide with me.

I need Thy presence every passing hour;
What but Thy grace can foil the tempter's power?
Who like Thyself my guide and stay can be?
Through cloud and sunshine, Lord, abide with me.

I fear no foe with Thee at hand to bless;
Ills have no weight and tears no bitterness;
Where is death's sting? Where, grave, thy victory?
I triumph still, if Thou abide with me.

Hold Thou Thy Cross before my closing eyes;
Shine through the gloom, and point me to the skies;
Heaven's morning breaks, and earth's vain shadows flee;
In life, in death, O Lord, abide with me.

CARDINAL NEWMAN
1801 ~ 1890

John Henry Newman was vicar of St Mary's Church, Oxford and with his friends Keble and Pusey was a leading member of the Oxford Movement. In 1833, after visiting Rome and being near to death of a fever in Sicily, he wrote this fine poem (which he never intended as a hymn) on his homeward journey to England when his ship was becalmed in the straits of Bonifacio. In it he expresses his agonies of doubt as to his future; nine years later he was received into the Roman Catholic Church.

In his Apologia Pro Vita Sua describing his religious development he tells how he came to write this poem.

John Bacchus Dykes

(1823 - 1876)

A HYMN FOR GUIDANCE

Lead, kindly Light, amid the encircling gloom,
    Lead Thou me on;
The night is dark, and I am far from home,
    Lead Thou me on.
Keep Thou my feet; I do not ask to see
The distant scene; one step enough for me.

I was not ever thus, nor prayed that Thou
    Shouldst lead me on;
I loved to choose and see my path; but now
    Lead Thou me on.
I loved the garish day, and, spite of fears,
Pride ruled my will: remember not past years.

So long Thy power hath blest me, sure it still
    Will lead me on,
O'er moor and fen, o'er crag and torrent, till
    The night is gone;
And with the morn those Angel faces smile
Which I have loved long since, and lost awhile.

ALFRED LORD TENNYSON 1809-1892

At the age of forty Tennyson succeeded Wordsworth as Poet Laureate and at last obtained her parents' consent to marry Emily Selwood. In the same year (1850) his poem "In Memoriam" was published and was an immediate success; it had taken him sixteen years to write and was in memory of his Cambridge friend Arthur Hallam.   Later he wrote Idylls of the King, poems about King Arthur, which were very popular.

   He received a peerage at the age of seventy-five. "Crossing the Bar" is considered one of his most moving poems; it is said that the idea came to him when towards the end of his life he was crossing the Solent with his son Hallam on his way to the Isle of Wight where he had a house.

Hubert Parry (1848-1918)

Sunset and evening star,
And one clear call for me!
And may there be no moaning of the bar
When I put out to sea.
But such a tide as moving seems asleep,
To full for sound and foam,
When that which drew from out the boundless deep
Turns again home.

Twilight and evening bell,
And after that the dark!
And may there be no sadness of farewell
When I embark:
For though from out our bourne of time and place
The flood may bear me far,
I hope to see my Pilot face to face
When I have crost the bar.

Crossing the Bar.   by Alfred Lord Tennyson

DEAN ALFORD 1810 – 1871

Henry Alford composed the famous processional hymn "Forward be our Watchword" first sung in Canterbury Cathedral where he was Dean, and he also wrote "Ten thousand times" which was sung at his funeral. He composed music for his hymns, but his greatest achievment is considered to be his Commentary on the Greek New Testament which became the standard work of its time.

This is his best loved hymn and is still widely used at Harvest Festival services.

George Elvey (1816-93)

HARVEST FESTIVAL

Come, ye thankful people, come,
Raise the song of harvest-home;
All is safely gathered in,
Ere the winter storms begin;
God our Maker doth provide
For our wants to be supplied;
Come to God's own temple come;
Raise the song of harvest-home.

All this world is God's own field
Fruit unto His praise to yield
Wheat and tares therein are sown,
Unto joy or sorrow grown;
Ripening with a wondrous power
Till the final harvest-hour:
Grant, O Lord of life, that we
Holy grain and pure may be.

For we know that Thou wilt come,
And wilt take Thy people home;
From Thy field wilt purge away
All that doth offend, that day;
And Thine angels charge at last
In the fire the tares to cast,
But the fruitful ears to store
In Thy garner evermore.

Come then, Lord of mercy come
Bid us sing Thy harvest-home:
Let Thy Saints be gathered in,
Free from sorrow, free from sin;
All upon the golden floor
Praising Thee for evermore;
Come with all Thy Angels come,
Bid us sing Thy harvest-home.

MRS ALEXANDER
1818 — 1895

Cecil Frances Alexander was the most successful of those who wrote hymns specifically for children. Although they were first intended for her Sunday School class they were later published (forty of them) in her _Hymns for Little Children_ in 1848, which ran to a hundred editions and was prefaced by John Keble. Of a kindly disposition she was loved by all with whom she came into contact. Her husband, a country clergyman, later became Bishop of Derry and then Archbishop of Armagh and Primate of All Ireland, but this elevation never deterred her from her ministry to the needy.

English Traditional Melody
arr. Martin Shaw

A HYMN FOR THE YOUNG

All things bright and beautiful,
　All creatures great and small,
All things wise and wonderful,
　The Lord God made them all.

Each little flower that opens,
　Each little bird that sings,
He made their glowing colours,
　He made their tiny wings.

The purple-headed mountain,
　The river running by,
The sunset, and the morning
　That brightens up the sky;

The cold wind in the winter,
　The pleasant summer sun,
The ripe fruits in the garden,
　He made them every one.

The tall trees in the greenwood,
　The meadows where we play,
The rushes by the water,
　We gather every day;

He gave us eyes to see them,
　And lips that we might tell,
How great is God Almighty,
　Who has made all things well.

MRS ALEXANDER
1818 – 1895

In 1850 Cecil Frances Humphreys married William Alexander, rector of a parish in co. Tyrone. As the rector's wife, her greatest joy was to visit the sick and needy. 'From one bed of sickness to another, from one sorrow to another, she went' wrote her husband in his biography of her; 'Christ was ever with her, and in her, and all felt her influence.' She wrote this hymn to try to explain to children something of the deeper meaning of Christianity.

William Horsley (1774-1858)

A HYMN FOR CHILDREN
by Mrs Alexander

There is a green hill far away,
　Without a city wall,
Where the dear Lord was crucified,
　Who died to save us all.

We may not know, we cannot tell
　What pains he had to bear,
But we believe it was for us
　He hung and suffered there.

He died that we might be forgiven,
　He died to make us good,
That we might go at last to heaven,
　Saved by His precious blood.

There was no other good enough
　To pay the price of sin;
He only could unlock the gate
　Of Heaven and let us in.

Oh dearly, dearly has He loved,
　And we must love Him too,
And trust in His redeeming blood,
　And try His works to do.

23

WILLIAM WHITING
1825 - 1878

In 1860, Whiting, while master at Winchester College Choristers' School, wrote this hymn which became the theme song of sailors; not only is it used in ships of the Royal Navy, but also in the American fleet, and a translation has been included in a hymn book of the French navy.

His fame rests entirely on this one hymn, and this may be partly due to the tune which Dykes at once wrote for it so that it could be included in the first edition of Hymns Ancient and Modern that came out the following year. Its rolling bass may well appeal to a nation of seafarers!

John Bacchus Dykes.
(1823 - 76)

A HYMN FOR THOSE AT SEA

Eternal Father, strong to save,
Whose arm hath bound the restless wave,
Who bidd'st the mighty ocean deep
Its own appointed limits keep:
O hear us when we cry to Thee
For those in peril on the sea.

O Christ, whose voice the waters heard
And hushed their raging at Thy word,
Who walkedst on the foaming deep,
And calm amid the storm did sleep:
O hear us when we cry to Thee
For those in peril on the sea.

O Holy Spirit, who didst brood
Upon the waters dark and rude,
And bid their angry tumult cease,
And give, for wild confusion, peace:
O hear us when we cry to Thee
For those in peril on the sea.

O Trinity of love and power,
Our brethren shield in danger's hour;
From rock and tempest, fire and foe,
Protect them wheresoe'er they go;
Thus evermore shall rise to Thee
Glad hymns of praise from land and sea.

ELEANOR FARJEON
1881 – 1965

The daughter of Benjamin Farjeon, the popular novelist, and grand-daughter of Joseph Jefferson, a famous American actor, Eleanor never went to school. She was educated at her home in London amongst the thousands of books owned by her father, whose custom it was, every Sunday, to give one to each of his four children to keep and to read as their own. At a very early age she wrote stories, poems and plays which she always gave first to her father for his opinion. Eleanor wrote over seventy children's books, many books of verse, and some novels for adults; she also contributed book reviews and verse to leading newspapers.

In 1955 she was awarded both the Carnegie and the Hans Andersen medals for a book of children's stories.

Gaelic Melody

Morning has broken
Like the first morning,
Blackbird has spoken
Like the first bird.
Praise for the singing,
Praise for the morning,
Praise for the springing
Fresh from the Word.

Sweet the rain's new fall
Sunlit from Heaven,
Like the first dewfall
On the first grass.
Praise for the sweetness
Of the wet garden,
Sprung in completeness
Where his feet pass.

Mine is the sunlight,
Mine is the morning
Born of the one light
Eden saw play.
Praise with elation,
Praise every morning,
God's re-creation
Of the new day.

JAN STRUTHER
1901 – 1953

Jan Struther is the pen name of Joyce Torrens, formed from the initial letter of her Christian name and the family surname of her mother, who before her marriage to Henry Torrens was the Hon. Dame Eva Anstruther. She was educated privately in London, and as early as 1917 began contributing poems and short stories to magazines. Her poems and essays were published in several volumes, but she is best known for her novel, _Mrs Miniver_. She was the wife of Anthony Maxtone Graham, and during the 1939-45 war lived with her two children in New York, where she was much in demand as a lecturer. Her second marriage, to A.K. Placzek, took place in 1948. This hymn was commissioned in 1931 for the hymn book _Songs of Praise_.

Irish Traditional Melody

A HYMN FOR A WORKING-DAY

Lord of all hopefulness, Lord of all joy,
Whose trust, ever childlike, no cares could destroy,
Be there at our waking and give us, we pray,
Your bliss in our hearts, Lord, at the break of
the day.

Lord of all eagerness, Lord of all faith,
Whose strong hands were skilled at the plane and
the lathe,
Be there at our labours and give us, we pray,
Your strength in our hearts, Lord, at the noon of the day.

Lord of all kindliness, Lord of all grace,
Your hands swift to welcome, your arms to
embrace,
Be there at our homing and give us, we pray,
Your love in our hearts, Lord, at the eve of the day.

Lord of all gentleness, Lord of all calm,
Whose voice is contentment, whose presence is balm,
Be there at our sleeping and give us, we pray,
Your peace in our hearts, Lord, at the end
of the day.